The SECRET WORLD of SPY Agencies

BY

SUSAN K. MITCHELL

THE SECRET WORLD OF SPIES

Enslow Publishers, Inc.

40 Industrial Road
Box 398
Berkeley Heights, NJ 07922
USA   http://www.enslow.com

For my wonderful parents, Robbie & Dub

Library of Congress Cataloging-in-Publication Data

Mitchell, Susan K.
   The secret world of spy agencies / Susan K. Mitchell.
      p. cm. — (The secret world of spies)
   Includes index.
   Summary: "Examines spy agencies in the United States and around the world, including
      the founding of these agencies, how they work, who works for them, and looks at
      specific agencies, such as the CIA, MI5, KGB, and BND"—Provided by publisher.
   ISBN 978-0-7660-3714-4
   1. Intelligence service—Juvenile literature. 2. Espionage—Juvenile literature. 3. Spies—
      Juvenile literature. I. Title.
   JF1525.I6M578 2012
   327.12—dc22
                                                              2010047601

Paperback ISBN 978-1-59845-352-2

Printed in China

052011 Leo Paper Group, Heshan City, Guangdong, China

10 9 8 7 6 5 4 3 2 1

To Our Readers: We have done our best to make sure all Internet Addresses in this book were active and appropriate when we went to press. However, the author and the publisher have no control over and assume no liability for the material available on those Internet sites or on other Web sites they may link to. Any comments or suggestions can be sent by e-mail to comments@enslow.com or to the address on the back cover.

Illustration Credits: © AF archive / Alamy, p. 23; AP Images, p. 17; AP Images / Alastair Grant, p. 21; AP Images / Charles Dharapak, p. 19; AP Images / Lionel Cironneau, p. 42; AP Images / Liu Heung Shing, p. 34; AP Images / PA Wire, p. 26; © Elena Korenbaum / iStockphoto.com, p. 35; Everett Collection, p. 24; © Frank Naylor / Alamy, p. 41; The Granger Collection, New York, p. 7; © INTERFOTO / Alamy, p. 38; Library of Congress, pp. 6, 10, 12, 14; © Mike Goldwater / Alamy, p. 31; © RIA Novosti / Alamy, p. 28; Shutterstock.com, pp. 3, 4, 32, 44; © Urbanmyth / Alamy, p. 40.

Cover Illustration: Mehau Kulyk / Photo Researchers, Inc. (background); Shutterstock .com (World wide binary vector drawing, lower right corner).

CONTENTS

Chapter 1

Secrets in Service

Behind every good spy is a strong spy agency. These organizations give spies the resources they need to do their job. Most of them are government agencies. These spy organizations are huge! There are thousands of people working at different jobs. All together, they work to make sure spies can complete their missions. No one spy can do his or her job alone.

The history of spies goes back many thousands of years, even as far back as ancient Greece. The history of spy agencies, however, does not. In fact, organized spy agencies are only a few hundred years old. Before the 1800s, most spying was done by small groups or individuals. They were not part of a government. Nor were they part of a military. Therefore, little is known about these earliest spies.

That began to change during the Civil War. At that time, the Pinkertons were at their peak. Allan Pinkerton and his brother, Robert, each entered the spy trade quite by accident. They were Scottish immigrants to the United States. Each brother had his own business. Allan had a barrel-making business. Robert had a railroad business. However, it would be spying that changed their lives.

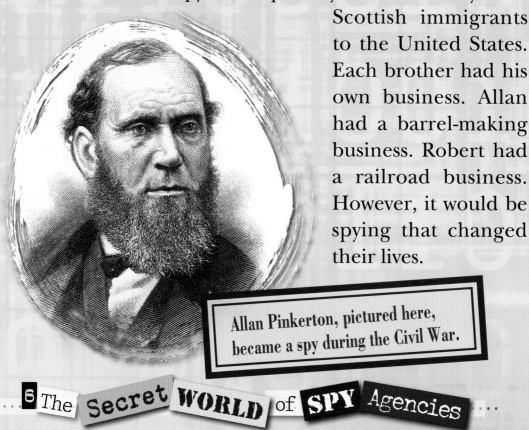

Allan Pinkerton, pictured here, became a spy during the Civil War.

We Never Sleep

Detectives are often called "private eyes." It is believed that this saying began with the Pinkerton agency. The logo for the agency was a large, open eye. The agency also used the words, "We never sleep." The agency still operates today. Now, it goes by the name Pinkerton Consulting & Investigations. Its logo is still a version of that open eye.

This is Pinkerton's National Detective Agency logo. It shows the open eye with the famous phrase "We never sleep."

PINKERTON'S NATIONAL DETECTIVE AGENCY.
We never sleep.
unsel for the Agency,
29 NASSAU ST. NEW YORK.

Masters of Spies

Both brothers seemed to have a knack for detective work. They were just naturals. Soon, they teamed up. Together, they formed Pinkerton's National Detective Agency. They worked to protect railroads and stagecoaches. During some railroad work, Allan claimed to discover a secret. It was a plot to kill President Abraham Lincoln in February 1861.

It is believed the Pinkertons' spy work may have helped save the president's life. President Lincoln was impressed. He decided to create an official secret service organization. It would serve the Union government. The main focus of the organization would be to find and shut down money counterfeiters. This was a huge problem at the time. Of course, Lincoln hired Allan Pinkerton because he had so much experience finding people who made counterfeit money. He had a good reputation and a great ability to find out information.

The agency also spied on the Confederacy during the Civil War. It gathered information to help the Union forces and President Lincoln. Allan Pinkerton acted as spymaster. The job made him

responsible for sending out spies who worked for him. He had a team of spies who worked to gather information on the Confederacy in the South.

Pinkerton made sure his spies had the information and protection they needed to do their job. He took their secrecy seriously. Very few people could get information on Pinkerton spies. Even their paychecks used only initials in order to protect the spies' identities.

The Tide Changes

By 1862, the Pinkertons were forced out of the secret service organization. They no longer worked for President Lincoln. Lafayette C. Baker took control of the agency. Unlike Pinkerton, Baker did not have a good reputation. He was very different from Pinkerton.

Baker did things the Pinkerton brothers would never have done. He terrorized some people and

Allan Pinkerton (left) and Abraham Lincoln stand together at a military camp during the Civil War. President Lincoln created a spy organization during the war. He made Pinkerton the spymaster.

SECRET FACT

The original secret service organization Lincoln created led to the beginning of today's United States Secret Service. It is a law enforcement agency that still exists today.

blackmailed others. He also threatened people to get information. Baker was ill equipped to run the secret service agency.

In 1865, President Lincoln was shot and killed. Lincoln's assasination happened on Baker's watch. In 1866, Baker was fired as head of the intelligence service. President Andrew Johnson claimed Baker was spying on the new president's office.

The early spy agencies of the Civil War directly led to a new way to use spies. They showed what a bit of organization could do. By 1880, the Office of Naval Intelligence was formed. In the same year, the Army's Military Intelligence Division was also created. There were many more changes to come.

SPY AGENCIES DOWN SOUTH

The Union did not have the only spy network during the Civil War. The southern Confederacy also had one. It was much less organized than the Union's spy agency. Most of the missions were done by one person or small groups. They were done without the Confederate government's guidance. Few of the spies communicated with each other. It was not nearly as effective as the Union's agency.

SURRAT.   BOOTH.   HAROLD.

War Department, Washington, April 20, 1865,

 # $100,000 REWARD!

THE MURDERER

Of our late beloved President, Abraham Lincoln,

IS STILL AT LARGE.

$50,000 REWARD

Will be paid by this Department for his apprehension, in addition to any reward offered by Municipal Authorities or State Executives.

$25,000 REWARD

Will be paid for the apprehension of JOHN H. SURRATT, one of Booth's Accomplices.

$25,000 REWARD

Will be paid for the apprehension of David C. Harold, another of Booth's accomplices.

LIBERAL REWARDS will be paid for any information that shall conduce to the arrest of either of the above named criminals, or their accomplices.

All persons harboring or secreting the said persons, or either of them, or aiding or assisting their concealment or escape, will be treated as accomplices in the murder of the President and the attempted assassination of the Secretary of State, and shall be subject to trial before a Military Commission and the punishment of DEATH.

Let the stain of innocent blood be removed from the land by the arrest and punishment of the murderers.

All good citizens are exhorted to aid public justice on this occasion. Every man should consider his own conscience charged with this solemn duty, and rest neither night nor day until it be accomplished.

EDWIN M. STANTON, Secretary of War.

DESCRIPTIONS.—BOOTH is Five Feet 7 or 8 inches high, slender build, high forehead, black hair, black eyes, and wears a heavy black moustache.

JOHN H. SURRAT is about 5 feet, 9 inches. Hair rather thin and dark; eyes rather light; no beard. Would weigh 145 or 150 pounds. Complexion rather pale and clear, with color in his cheeks. Wore light clothes of fine quality. Shoulders square; cheek bones rather prominent; chin narrow; ears projecting at the top; forehead rather low and square, but broad. Parts his hair on the right side; neck rather long. His lips are firmly set. A slim man.

DAVID C. HAROLD is five feet six inches high, hair dark, eyes dark, eyebrows rather heavy, full face, nose short, hand short and fleshy, feet small, instep high, round bodied, naturally quick and active, slightly closes his eyes when looking at a person.

NOTICE.—In addition to the above, State and other authorities have offered rewards amounting to almost one hundred thousand dollars, making an aggregate of about TWO HUNDRED THOUSAND DOLLARS.

President Lincoln was killed on April 14, 1865. This reward poster was issued for the murderers after his death.

Protecting the Homeland

Spy agencies in the United States have changed quite a bit. They have come a long way since those Pinkerton days. Today, the main spy agency in the United States is the Central Intelligence Agency (CIA). However, it was not the first American spy agency. The CIA went through many changes on the way to becoming the agency it is today.

World War II changed many things in America. It also changed the way the U.S. government viewed spying. As President Lincoln had discovered many years earlier, spying was critical to keeping our country safe. During World War II, President Franklin D. Roosevelt saw the need for a formal organized spy agency. He set out to create one.

The result was the Office of Strategic Services (OSS). It was created in 1942. The new agency helped greatly during the war. However, after the war ended, the new president, Harry S. Truman, closed the OSS. By 1945, it had been abandoned. The government still had not figured out the usefulness of a spy agency during times of peace. That would soon change.

President Harry S. Truman closed the OSS. However, the U.S. government soon created a new intelligence agency.

Ready and Waiting

The best offense is often a good defense. Some advisers to President Truman realized this idea. They knew that spying is not only helpful during war. It can be a huge key in preventing attacks as well. In 1946, Truman created the Central Intelligence Group (CIG). It was another step toward today's CIA evolution.

There was a big difference between the CIG and previous agencies. In the past, spy agencies had been connected to the military. The CIG, however, was a civilian-run agency. That meant it was not run by the military.

This early agency did have a few problems. In 1947, the CIG was shut down. A better agency was formed to take its place. That agency was the CIA. One spy important to its beginnings was James Jesus Angleton. He was one of the early CIA's most influential spies. He was also one of the most controversial.

Making the Mossad

The Mossad is Israel's version of the CIA. It is their main spy agency. The Mossad was created in 1951. Angleton was a key player in its formation, too. Since its early days, the Mossad has worked closely with the CIA. They often share information. The Mossad helps the CIA keep track of their common enemies. The CIA now works with many spy agencies around the world to track down the same enemies.

Spy Catcher

With Angleton, it is hard to separate fact from fiction. His history with the CIA is as much legend as it is truth. What is certain, however, is that Angleton began his career in the OSS during World War II. In 1943, he traveled to England to train with the Military Intelligence Section 5, known as MI5. That was one of England's two spy agencies. With the MI5, Angleton showed a talent in counterintelligence.

James Angleton is one of the most influential spies in the history of the CIA.

SECRET FACT

The CIA seal has a sixteen-pointed star on it. It stands for its search for intelligence all over the world.

By 1954, Angleton was the head of the CIA's counterintelligence unit. He held this position for twenty years. One of his main jobs was to track down Soviet moles. Moles are also called double agents. They are enemy agents that pretend to work for the CIA. Angleton became an expert at catching these Soviet spies.

He carried out this task with obsessive focus. So much so, that many in the CIA complained that Angleton lost sight of other issues. They believed Angleton to be paranoid. Things were getting out of control. By 1974, he was asked to resign. Angleton did so reluctantly. For good or bad, his twenty years of work would forever leave its mark on the CIA.

Only One Piece of the Puzzle

The CIA cannot do it all alone. It relies on other American agencies to help. The National Security Agency (NSA) is actually larger than the CIA. It handles intelligence like codes and code breaking. The Secret Service protects the president and other politicians. The FBI handles matters inside the United States. It is not a spy agency, but it does use intelligence-gathering techniques in law enforcement. In all, there are more than fifteen different agencies in the United States that contribute intelligence!

One of the main jobs of the Secret Service is to protect the president and the first family. Secret Service agents stand watch as President Barack Obama and First Lady Michelle Obama walk from Marine One helicopter in Baden-Baden, Germany.

Spying Across the Pond

One of the oldest organized spy agencies in the world began in England. It was formed even before the American CIA. It goes back all the way to 1909 and went by several names. The agency began as MI6. Like many early spy agencies, MI6 was directly connected to the military. In fact, MI stands for military intelligence.

In its early years, the MI6 was only one of England's two military spy agencies. MI6 handled things for the British navy. MI5 handled the army's intelligence. MI5 was assigned to deal with security issues inside England. MI6 handled issues regarding other countries.

For several years, these two agencies worked side by side. After World War I, they began to separate. MI6 even had a name change. It was renamed the Secret Intelligence Service, or SIS for short. Today, SIS is the official name of the agency. Many people often use MI6, however.

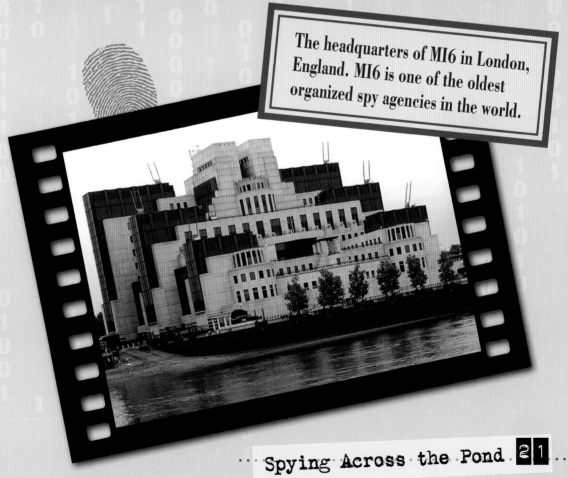

The headquarters of MI6 in London, England. MI6 is one of the oldest organized spy agencies in the world.

The early MI5 had one main focus. Its job was to find German spies inside England.

SECRET FACT

British Super Spy

One of MI6's biggest weapons in the spy game was Sidney Reilly. He was such an amazing spy that the line between his real life and that of fiction is not clear. It is believed that Reilly was born in Russia in 1874. Then, his name was Georgi Rosenblum. There are many versions of how he came to be one of MI6's top spies.

After ending up on the bad side of the Russian government, Rosenblum faked his own death. He fled Russia. For several years, he worked as a spy for other countries. Eventually, he ended up in England. There, he became Sidney Reilly.

His adventurous nature lent itself to spying for MI6. He changed identities as easily as changing clothes. Reilly seemed ready for even the most dangerous missions. In 1918, he was supposedly sent to kill Russian leader Vladimir Lenin. The mission was never completed. Another spy beat

Reilly there. The mission had seriously damaged his cover. Reilly had been exposed. The Russians executed him in 1925.

Still Going Strong

It has been about one hundred years since MI6 was formed. In that time, it has tried to maintain the secrecy surrounding its spy agency. Its objectives have changed over the years. MI6 has chased Nazis. Its spies pursued communists. Today, those threats are no longer around. New threats, however, have taken their place.

This photo of Sidney Reilly was taken in 1924. A year later, he was executed.

Spies by the Letters

The SIS does not waste time coming up with complicated code names for its spymaster. The agency prefers to use letters. The first head of MI6 was Captain Sir Mansfield Cumming. He used the code name "C." Vernon Kell was the first head of MI5. He was referred to as "K." Since then, every SIS director has used "C" as his code name. The code name "K," however, was not used again. These code names even worked their way into fiction. In the James Bond movies, "Q" is the code name for the agent who designs Bond's weapons and gadgets.

The British SIS used single letters as code names for its spymasters. This trend carried over into films. Agent "Q" created the gadgets used by James Bond. Agent Q, played here by Desmond Llewelyn (left), appears with actor Sean Connery as James Bond in a movie called *You Only Live Twice* in 1967.

The modern MI6 has refocused its energy as many spy agencies around the world have. Now, it focuses on battling terrorism. Terrorists can be found all over the world. The threat can even come from within an agency's country. The MI6 also works with other spy agencies to stop governments and other groups who try to develop dangerous weapons of mass destruction.

Today, England is also more open about the mysterious MI6. In 1994, the British government passed the Intelligence Services Act. This made MI6 more visible. It now has to answer more to Parliament, England's law-making branch of government. More is known about MI6 than ever before. It is certain, however, that there are still many secrets lurking below the surface. What else could be expected from the oldest spy agency in the world?

SECRET FACT

Sidney Reilly spoke seven languages! It is also believed he is the inspiration for the fictional spy James Bond.

A Fox in the Henhouse

MI6 has not been without scandal or embarrassment. Its most famous fiasco was that of the Cambridge Five spy ring. Double agent, Kim Philby, and several of his companions worked for MI6. Unknown to the agency, they were also working for the Soviet Union. Philby was stealing MI6 secrets and selling them.

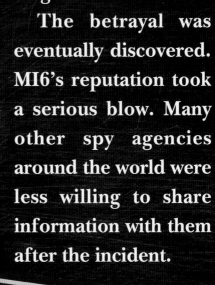

The betrayal was eventually discovered. MI6's reputation took a serious blow. Many other spy agencies around the world were less willing to share information with them after the incident.

Kim Philby, part of the Cambridge Five spy ring, betrayed the MI6 by giving British secrets to the Soviet Union.

Chapter

4

On the Dark Side

Some spy agencies have a fearsome reputation. The Russian KGB is known for deadly spies. In many books and movies, KGB agents are often the bad guys. There is some truth to that reputation. Since its beginning in 1917, the KGB used violence as a spy tool.

Like many other spy agencies, the KGB went through several name changes over the years. The KGB began as the Cheka. In 1922, it was called the GPU. Soviet leader Joseph Stalin took control of the GPU. He used it as his personal agency. It became an organization of terror, and it routinely used force to get what it needed. The GPU did not hesitate to attack or kill those who opposed Stalin.

Joseph Stalin (right) smiles for a photo with Felix Dzerzhinsky, the founder of the Cheka, the first organized spy agency in Russia. Stalin changed the name of the Cheka to the GPU and turned it into an organization of terror for his personal use.

The KGB was a constant threat to the U.S. Embassy in the Soviet Union. The U.S. regularly looked for bugs, or listening devices, inside the embassy.

There were several more name changes over the years. But no matter what the name, Stalin used the spy agency to crush his opponents. It remained under his control. For almost thirty years, the agency was one of the most feared spy agencies in the world. That changed after Stalin's death in 1953. The following year, it was renamed the KGB. Over the next few years, the KGB went through huge changes. Its reputation, however, had been solidified. It was a force to be feared.

On the Inside

The Cold War-era KGB had abandoned some of its more deadly methods. It was still dangerous, but the KGB was more secretive about it. The agency and the spies in it were a mystery. The spies were such shadowy figures that today little is known about specific KGB agents. There are few names that stand out in history.

The few agents that are well known are not Russian KGB agents at all. They are the American spies that the KGB used against the United States. The KGB became very good at recruiting double agents. It found Americans who were willing to betray their country. Some of these traitors were tempted by money. Others were threatened or blackmailed by the KGB. Either way, this allowed the KGB to break through to the highest-level agencies in the United States. KGB double agents even worked inside the CIA and FBI.

During the Cold War, the KGB was America's greatest threat. There seemed to be almost no secret it could not uncover. The KGB found out top U.S. military and science secrets. The KGB went after anything it could use against the United States. The KGB was willing to do anything to get those secrets. However, that era, too, would come to an end.

The KGB was very secretive. Today, very little is known about specific KGB agents. This KGB officer uses a forensic kit at a KGB training school in Moscow, Russia.

Silent in the Shadows

The KGB was not the only spy agency in the Soviet Union. There was a larger agency as well. It was the GRU. Created in 1918, this agency still exists today. The GRU handled mostly military intelligence. It was a silent and shadowy agency that kept a low profile.

The GRU and KGB often fought in their own power struggle. Unlike the KGB, the GRU was not reorganized after the fall of the Soviet Union. It still operates in Russia.

This is the headquarters of the former KGB in Moscow.

Making Peace

In the 1980s, big changes occurred in the Soviet Union. A new president took power. His name was Mikhail Gorbachev. The changes included improving relations with the United States. He began to change the KGB. By 1991, the Soviet Union of the past was no more. The Cold War was over.

These changes did not sit well with the KGB. In 1991, the head of the KGB tried to remove Soviet president Gorbachev from power. That type of attempt is called a coup (pronounced, koo). It was unsuccessful. The event proved to be a step toward the end of the KGB as it was known. It was also the end of the Soviet Union.

SECRET FACT

Some former KGB agents are still in power in Russia. Former president and current prime minister, Vladimir Putin, was a KGB agent from 1975 to 1990.

Russian president Boris Yeltsin (with fist in the air) officially ended the KGB. He broke it up into several different agencies.

The communist Soviet Union was now a united democratic Russia. Russian president Boris Yeltsin took steps to finally eliminate the KGB forever. Yeltsin broke it into several different agencies. One of which is the FSB. After the Cold War, relations between Russia and the United States improved. But the CIA and the FSB still have trust issues today.

Break on Through to the Other Side

The KGB was great at using double agents against the United States. They did fall victim to betrayal, too. That threat came from defectors. A defector is a person who leaves his or her country and goes to another country. At times, some Soviet agents did this. They left the Soviet Union for America or England.

Oleg Gordievsky (gor-dee-YEV-skee) was such an agent. He was a high-ranking KGB official. He was also a double agent working for the British MI6. Gordievsky disliked the way the KGB operated. Over the years, he provided MI6 with valuable information. It is believed that an American double agent, Aldrich Ames, blew his cover. Gordievsky had to flee for his life. He defected to England in 1985.

Chapter 5

Rising From the Ashes

Spy agencies are by nature very mysterious. It is that shadow of secrecy, which allows them to do their jobs. Some of today's best spy agencies have risen out of the dark shadows of a dangerous past. The German spy agency BND is one of those. Today, it is a friend of the CIA. They work together and share information. The BND's past, however, is far murkier.

In the 1930s, the Nazi movement was in full force in Germany. Adolf Hitler had established an intelligence agency. One of the men in charge of intelligence gathering was Reinhard Gehlen. He was a high-ranking general in the Nazi military. His focus was gathering information on the Soviet Union.

Gehlen was great at his job. He was not, however, a loyal supporter of Hitler. In 1945, Gehlen surrendered to U.S. forces. He knew they were interested in the Soviets. He used his information as a bargaining chip. Soon after that, the Gehlen Organization was created. Over the next several years, it worked closely with the CIA.

SECRET FACT

Reinhard Gehlen took part in a failed plot to kill Adolf Hitler. His role was minor, however. He covered up his involvement and escaped execution.

Reinhard Gehlen was in charge of intelligence gathering in Germany during World War II. After the war, he created the Gehlen Organization.

Torn in Two

In 1956, the Gehlen Organization became the BND. Reinhard Gehlen stayed on as its chief. The new BND was the central intelligence agency of West Germany. After World War II, Germany was divided into two countries: West Germany and East Germany. They were enemies.

Law of the Land

Few, if any, intelligence agencies act as law enforcement. They can spy, but they cannot make arrests. Agencies like the CIA, SIS, or BND only collect information. Their spies uncover secrets that are then turned over to law enforcement. Then it is up to law enforcement agencies to use that information properly. In the United States, the FBI is one of those agencies. The FBI can use what the CIA finds out to carry out investigations and make arrests. Law enforcement agencies rely on their relationships with intelligence agencies. They have to work together to get the job done.

The East Germans had their own intelligence agency. It had a far more terrifying reputation than the BND. It was called the Stasi. The agency was created a few years before the BND in 1950. The Stasi acted much like the Soviet KGB. It also worked closely with the KGB. The Stasi was even allowed to have bases inside the Soviet Union.

The Stasi kept a close watch on all East German citizens. This is a former Stasi prison in Berlin, Germany.

It has been estimated that the Stasi had one agent for every 166 citizens. That made it one of the largest spy networks in the world. The Stasi spied on almost everyone. It kept files on thousands of citizens. No one was above suspicion. The Stasi watched every move an East German made. It was a culture of fear.

When the Wall Fell

The BND and the Stasi were constantly fighting against each other. One advantage the Stasi had was in planting double agents. Almost all of the

informants the BND had working in East Germany were actually double agents controlled by the Stasi. This would last for nearly forty years. By 1990, the East German government fell. Germany was reunited and the Stasi was gone.

With the Stasi eliminated, only the BND was left. It became the main intelligence agency for all of Germany. It was free to continue its partnership with the United States. The CIA and BND routinely share information. Other countries have good relations with the BND as well.

TOP SECRET

The Stasi had many double agents working for the agency. Those double agents used many secret spy tools, such as this infrared listening device hidden in a car door.

Germans celebrate the dismantling of the Berlin Wall that divided East Germany and West Germany. When Germany was reunited, the Stasi was gone forever.

Thousands of Stasi informants were under the age of eighteen. They were usually forced to become informants.

SECRET FACT

Today, the BND regularly cooperates with the United States against terrorism. It has a strong reputation as a cooperative agency. It also works with other intelligence agencies inside Germany. The BND has successfully shed the dark past of its Nazi and Stasi roots.

SECRET FACT

Behind the Scenes

Spy agencies are the key to successful spies and missions. They are the center of information and support for agents. Without that support, spies would not be able to do their job. No one spy agency can work alone. Each agency within the United States and many agencies around the world rely on each other. These agencies provide technology. They give protection. These agencies are full of members willing to put their lives on the line to help agents finish a mission.

SPIES Like Who?

A CAREER AS A SPY MASTER

The actual job title of a person who manages a special agent is Collection Management Officer (CMO). He or she works for the National Clandestine Service (NCS), which is part of the CIA. It is the job of CMOs to guide agents. CMOs also act as go-betweens for the agents and those who need the information the agents discover. Many CMOs have been agents before. They must have a college degree with excellent grades. They usually work in Washington, D.C. CMOs may make between $53,000 and $81,000 each year.

Would you like a career as a spymaster? You must go to college and study hard. A career in the CIA could be waiting for you.

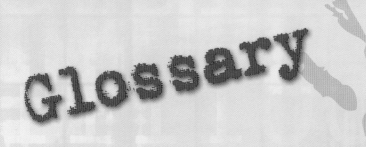

Glossary

civilian—A person not connected to the military.

counterfeiters—People who create counterfeit, or fake, money.

counterintelligence—Preventing an enemy from gathering intelligence.

immigrants—People who move to another country to live.

informants—One who is a source of information.

moles—In espionage, a person who works as a double agent to find out enemy information.

paranoid—Suffering from excessive worry or suspicion.

spymaster—A person who handles and directs spies.

traitors—Those who betray, or go against, their country.

To Find Out More

Books

Burgan, Michael. **Spies and Traitors: Stories of Masters of Deception.** Mankato, Minn.: Capstone Press, 2010.

Bursztynski, Sue. **It's True! This Book Is Bugged.** Toronto: Annick Press, 2007.

Janeczko, Paul B. **The Dark Game: True Spy Stories.** Sommerville, Mass.: Candlewick Press, 2010.

O'Shei, Tim. **Spy Basics.** Mankato, Minn.: Capstone Press, 2008.

Wagner, Heather Lehr. **The Central Intelligence Agency.** New York: Chelsea House Publications, 2007.

Internet Addresses

Central Intelligence Agency Kids' Page
  <https://www.cia.gov/kids-page/index.html>

Intelligence Search: Spy Agencies of the World
  <http://www.intelligencesearch.com/
    intelligence-agencies.html>

Office of the Director of National
    Intelligence: Intelligence Community Agency
    Kids' Pages
  <http://www.dni.gov/kids.htm>

Index